HEALTHY SNACKS
FOR KIDS

TARLA DALAL

India's # 1 Cookery Author

S&C
SANJAY & CO.
MUMBAI

Fifth Printing : 2011

ISBN : 978-8-189491-25-3

Price: Rs. 99/-

Published & Distributed by : **Sanjay & Company**

353/A-1, Shah & Nahar Industrial Estate, Dhanraj Mill Compound, Lower Parel (W), Mumbai - 400 013. INDIA.
Tel. : (91-22) 4345 2400 • Fax : (91-22) 2496 5876 • E-mail : sanjay@tarladalal.com • Website : www.tarladalal.com

UK and USA customers can call us on :
UK : 02080029533   •   USA : 213-634-1406
For books, Membership on **tarladalal.com**, Subscription for **Cooking & More** and Recipe queries
Timing : Monday to Friday 9.30 a.m. to 6.00 p.m. (IST) and Saturday 9.30 a.m. to 1.30 p.m. (IST)
Local call charges applicable

Recipe Research & Production Design Arati Fedane Umaima Abdulally	**Nutritionist** Nisha Katira Sapna Kamdar	**Photography** Jignesh Jhaveri	**Designed by** Satyamangal Rege	**Copy Editor** Ashvina Vakil
	Food Styling Shubhangi Dhaimade	**Typesetting** Adityas Enterprises	**Printed by :** Minal Sales Agencies, Mumbai	

BULK PURCHASES :Tarla Dalal Cookbooks are ideal gifts. If you are interested in buying more than 500 assorted copies of Tarla Dalal Cookbooks at special prices, please contact us at 91-22-4345 2400 or email : sanjay@tarladalal.com

INTRODUCTION

S nacks are an important part of your child's daily food intake. Well-planned healthy snacks can help not only to bridge the gap between meals and provide necessary nutrients, but also to encourage your child to develop good eating habits.

In consultation with my efficient team of chefs and nutritionists, I thought of bringing out a special book on **Healthy Snacks for Kids**. The book contains simple and healthy snack ideas that are quick to put together and eat, and also offer important nutrients and energy in each delicious bite. A total of **41** healthy snacks have been clubbed under four interesting sections: *Filling Snacks* - nutritionally well balanced mini meals just big enough to fill a child's tiny stomach; *Jar Snacks* - snacks that can be made in advance and stored; *Finger Foods* - interesting foods for little fingers; and *Sweet Treats* - delicious snacks to satisfy your child's sweet tooth in a healthy way.

We have used a range of healthy ingredients like soyabean, *paneer*, whole wheat bread, vegetables and fruits to create appetising snacks such as *Crunchy Soyabean Snack, page 46, Pahadi Paneer Tikkas, page 62*, and *Strawberry Stew with Banana Custard, page 97*. Healthy cooking methods like baking and steaming have helped re-invent traditionally fat-laden snacks such as *Tandoori Paneer Pizzas, page 16, Nutritious Burger, page 27, Quick Mini Soya Dosas, page 86 and Nutritious Chaklis, page 50*.

Different shapes and colours have been suggested to make the delicacies more appealing to the children, as done in *Potato Pops, page 64, Nutritious Idlis, page 24 and Fruit Ices, page 90 etc*. I am sure these healthy snacks will not only satisfy your child's frequent hunger pangs but also reduce mindless nibbling on calorie-laden snacks.

Happy and Healthy Snacking!

Regards

CONTENTS

❧ Snacking for Kids

Snacks are mini-meals that help keep us going until lunch or dinner. Children seem more inclined to snacking than adults and can often get addicted to a range of tasty but distinctly unhealthy snacking options such as chips, cookies and aerated drinks. Most mothers today find it really difficult to ensure that their kids eat a selection of healthy snacks. However, weaning children off unhealthy snacking is not so difficult all it requires is a little advance planning, and the time and patience to replace store-bought goodies with homemade nutritious ones.

So what makes a good snack? According to me, a good snack is one that is well balanced and nutrient-dense. This means that each bite contributes to the child's intake of healthy foods. Six nutrients are needed to maintain a growing and healthy body - carbohydrates, protein, fat, minerals, vitamins and water. To meets a child's requirement of these nutrients just ensure a healthy blend of food groups like cereals, pulses, dairy products, fruits and vegetables. This does not mean you have to include all these in the same snack, but try and cover at least two to three food groups at a time, and divide the rest throughout the day.

❧ Ten Benefits of Healthy Snacking

1. Bridges the gap between meals.
2. Satisfies the limited appetite of children who have small stomachs and need to eat often.
3. Contributes to 20% of a day's energy and nutrient requirements.
4. Prevents bingeing on junk foods and excessive weight gain early in life.
5. Offers a variety from all food groups.

6. Keeps children energetic and less grouchy throughout the day
7. Enhances intellectual development.
8. Fosters bone development, enhances immunity, and reduces susceptibility to diseases.
9. Helps to introduce good eating etiquette in children.
10. Exposes children to the different shapes, colours and textures of food.

☯ A Few Snack Time Tips

Making a healthy snack for kids that also tastes good is not a simple task. Here are some pointers:

☺ Plan and prepare quick, easy and kid-friendly snacks. Don't be swayed by advertising.

☺ Experiment with whole grains like whole wheat flour, whole wheat pasta, rice, and oats instead of opting for refined flour *(maida)* as much of the goodness in the latter is lost in the process of refining.

☺ Introduce a variety of snacks to prevent children from getting bored.

☺ Try and combine your child's favourite food with the one s(he) doesn't care for as much. This helps him/her adapt to new tastes more easily.

☺ Foods in different sizes and shapes often appeal to children, so occasionally serve them *rotis, parathas*, fruits and vegetables cut into squares or ovals, or in the shape of a letter or number.

☺ Presentation counts - serve snacks in brightly coloured plates.

☺ Keep healthy beverages such as fresh juices and soyamilk in the refrigerator and encourage your children to pack them into their bags before leaving the house.

☺ Children are good imitators. Set an example by inculcating healthy eating habits yourself.

- ☺ Involve your little ones in the snack creation process whenever possible: two-year-olds can peel bananas, put bread in a toaster, or arrange apple and cheese slices; three- to five-year-olds can cut soft foods and make sandwiches, pour liquids, shape dough etc.
- ☺ When shopping, let children pick out fruits, vegetables and cheese of their choice. They will be more interested in eating these foods if they have been involved in selecting them.
- ☺ Teach children to read food labels and help them choose healthy snacks from store shelves.
- ☺ To help your children choose healthy snacks, make charts with lists of foods within each food group and teach them to select foods from at least two different groups. Use pictures or words, depending on the age of your children.

☯ NO-No's of Snacking

- ☺ Avoid high sugar, fatty and salty snacks such as candy, chips, biscuits, soft drinks etc. Check out *Whole Wheat, Walnut and Raisin Cookies,* page 42 and *Granola Bars,* page 48, for some nourishing snack options.
- ☺ Do not let children nibble constantly during the day. Offer snacks at regular times such as mid-morning and mid-afternoon.
- ☺ Ban snacking in front of the television to prevent children from overeating or undereating.
- ☺ If your child occasionally refuses a snack, don't worry s(he) will definitely compensate for it in the next meal.

And do remember your children's snacking habits aren't going to change overnight. Look for positive changes over weeks and months. Teaching your children to make healthy snack choices today will help your whole family reap a lifetime of benefits.

☻ Quick Snacking Ideas

How often have you stood in front of your fridge/pantry/freezer waiting for a healthy snack idea to leap out at you? One that your kids will actually eat? When it doesn't, you probably resort to whatever you have on hand, healthy or not. Here are some essentials that you can stock in your freezer, pantry and fridge along with some quick recipe ideas.

What to stock

In the refrigerator

Fruits and vegetables that your child likes	*Idli* or *dosa* batter
Fresh curds	Salsa or any homemade dip
Paneer (cottage cheese)	Fresh juices
Boiled potatoes	Soyamilk
Chapati dough	

In the pantry

Popcorn	Cereals - preferably high fibre, low sugar varieties
Baked *chaklis, Chivda*	*Crackers
Nacho chips	Nuts
Chikki	Dried fruits
Honey	Barbeque sauce
Whole wheat pasta	*Tomato ketchup
Poha (beaten rice)	*Soup packets
Schezuan sauce	Whole wheat bread

In the freezer

Frozen fresh fruit purée	Ice-cream
Grated cheese	*Half cooked *chapatis*
Pizza sauce	*Chutneys*

* These foods are to be used moderately, once or twice in 15 days.

Easy Recipe Ideas

1. A fresh fruit salad with honey or curd dressing is a great idea in summer. Flavour the curd with fresh fruit purée or juice.
2. Cut vegetables into strips and serve with salsa or any other dip.
3. Occasionally fried *paneer* cubes taste great. Alternatively, mash the *paneer* and mix with green chutney / schezuan sauce / barbeque sauce or even *chaat masala* to make yummy fillings for sandwiches or *chapati* rolls.
4. Use boiled potatoes to whip up the ever-popular *aloo parathas* or make baked potatoes, potato wedges, *aloo chaat* etc. at a moment's notice. Mashed potatoes can be used to make fillings for grilled sandwiches.
5. Use *idli* batter to make regular *idlis* or vegetable *handva*, vegetable-stuffed *idlis* or mini *idlis* tossed in *masalas*.

6. Save jar snacks like popcorn, *chaklis,* nacho chips, corn flakes, nuts, dried fruit, and *chikki* for absolute emergencies when your child is totally famished and you don't have time to make a snack.

7. Though instant soup powders are laden with preservatives, you can use them occasionally if fortified with milk, fresh vegetables, etc.

8. Purées of seasonal fruits like strawberries and peaches and freeze. You can use this to whip up milkshakes.

9. Defrost frozen *chapatis* and use to make *quesadillas, chapati* rolls, *chapati* pizzas etc.

10. Mix some cereal or popcorn, dried fruits, nuts, seeds and perhaps some chocolate bits, serve with warm or chilled milk for a nutritious snack.

11. Grate little cheese over some nacho chips or toasted bread, and zap them in the microwave for about 5 minutes.

12. Ice cream always makes a yummy treat. Add chopped fresh fruit to enhance its nutritional value. Alternatively can blend fresh fruits with the ice-cream in a mixer to make rich and creamy smoothies.

So get ready to surprise your little darlings when they get home from school by whipping up many more yummy healthy snacks!

FILLING SNACKS

Curried Beans Pasta

Rich in
Vitamin A,
Potassium
& Fibre

Pasta is always a hit with children, and they will enjoy this tempting curried beans concoction.

Preparation time: 20 minutes.   Cooking time: 15 minutes.   Serves 4.

2 cups small whole wheat pasta (macaroni, fussilli, farfalle, etc.)
¼ cup soaked lima beans (*pavta*)
2 to 3 peppercorns
1 bayleaf (*tejpatta*)
¼ cup finely chopped onions
1 tsp finely chopped garlic
1 cup finely chopped tomatoes
2 tbsp tomato ketchup
1 tbsp fresh cream
1 tbsp butter

Salt to taste

1. Put plenty of water to boil, add the oil and salt. Add the pasta and cook till just done. Drain well and refresh in cold water. Drain again and keep aside.
2. Peel the soaked lima beans and boil in salted water till done. Drain, peel and keep aside.
3. Melt the butter in a pan and add the peppercorns and bayleaf.
4. Add the onions and garlic and sauté till the onions turn translucent.
5. Add the tomatoes and cook, mashing continuously with the back of a wooden spoon.
6. Add the cooked beans, tomato ketchup, cream, pasta and salt and heat while mixing gently.
   Serve hot.

Handy tip: If lima beans are not available, replace them with *rajma* (kidney beans).

Nutritive values per serving

Energy	Protein	Carbohydrates	Fat	Vitamin A	Potassium	Fibre
124 cal	3.4 gm	15.9 gm	5.1 gm	293.9 mcg	118.7 mg	1.2 gm

Tandoori Paneer Pizzas

Rich in Protein, Iron & Zinc

A protein-packed paneer topping gives a healthy twist to this all-time favourite with kids.

Preparation time: 30 minutes.   Cooking time: 3 to 5 minutes.   Serves 4.
Baking temperature: 200°C (400°F)   Baking time: 30 minutes.

2 nos. 200 mm. (8") whole wheat pizza bases
2 tbsp tomato ketchup
½ cup grated mozzarella cheese

For the *tandoori paneer* topping
1 cup *paneer* (cottage cheese) cubes
¼ cup capsicum cubes
¼ cup deseeded and cubed tomatoes
¼ cup onion cubes
1 tbsp fresh cream

To be mixed into a marinade
½ cup fresh thick curds (*dahi*)
1 tsp chilli powder
½ tsp dried Kasuri methi (*dried fenugreek leaves*), roasted and powdered
1 tsp ginger-garlic paste
½ tsp *garam masala*
1 tsp butter
Salt to taste

Other ingredients
½ tsp butter for greasing and glazing

For the *tandoori paneer* filling
1. Marinate the *paneer*, capsicum and tomato cubes in the prepared marinade for about 30 minutes.
2. Heat the butter in a saucepan, add the onion cubes and sauté for some time.
3. Add the marinated *paneer*, capsicum and tomatoes, and fresh cream and simmer for 3 to 5 minutes.
4. Remove from the fire and allow to cool.
5. Divide into 2 equal portions. Keep aside.

How to proceed
1. Place one pizza base on a greased baking tray.
2. Spread some tomato ketchup on it.
3. Spread half the *tandoori paneer* filling over the base.
4. Sprinkle half the cheese on top.
5. Bake in a pre-heated oven at 200°C (400°F) for 10 to 15 minutes or till the base is evenly browned and the cheese melts.
6. Repeat with the remaining ingredients to make another pizza. Serve hot.

Nutritive values per serving

Energy	Protein	Carbohydrates	Fat	Iron	Zinc
431 cal	**16.0 gm**	46.3 gm	20.0 gm	**2.9 mg**	**1.7 mg**

Veggie Submarines

Rich in Iron & Zinc

Picture on facing page.

Whole wheat hot dog rolls combine with soya granules and vegetables to make healthy submarines that will disappear in a flash!

Preparation time: 10 minutes.   Cooking time: 5 minutes.   Makes 6 submarines.
Baking temperature: 200°C (400°F).   Baking time: 15 minutes.

6 hot dog rolls (brown bread, lightly buttered)
¼ cup soya granules
1 tsp corn flour
¼ cup milk
1 tsp dry red chilli flakes
1 cup chopped and boiled mixed vegetables (French beans, carrots, green peas, potatoes, cauliflower, etc.)
2 tsp tomato ketchup

2 tsp butter
Salt and freshly crushed pepper to taste

For the topping
2 tsp grated cooking cheese

VEGGIE SUBMARINES : Recipe above. →

1. Slit each roll horizontally and toast lightly in a pre-heated oven or on a *tava* (griddle) for about 5 minutes. Keep aside.
2. Soak the soya granules in salted hot water for about 5 minutes. Drain and squeeze out all the water. Keep aside.
3. Dissolve the corn flour in the milk and keep aside.
4. Heat the butter in a non-stick pan, add the chilli flakes, boiled vegetables, salt and pepper and mix well.
5. Add the soya granules, tomato ketchup, milk-corn flour mixture and mix again. Cook for about 2 to 3 minutes.
6. Remove from the flame and keep aside.
7. Stuff each roll with a little of the prepared filling.
8. Sprinkle the grated cheese and grill in a pre-heated oven at 200°C (400°F) for 8 to 10 minutes or till the cheese melts.
   Serve hot.

Nutritive values per submarine

Energy	Protein	Carbohydrates	Fat	Iron	Zinc
209 cal	7.7 gm	36.2 gm	3.5 gm	**2.7 mg**	**1.1 mg**

Chapati Rolls

Rich in
Protein,
Calcium &
Folic Acid

This recipe makes a filling and balanced snack in itself. Chapatti provides energy giving carbohydrates; soya rolls are rich sources of protein and calcium whereas vegetables provide vitamins and fibre.

Preparation time: 30 minutes.   Cooking time: 30 minutes.   Makes 6 rolls.

6 *chapatis*, recipe below
3 tbsp chilli sauce (optional)
¼ cup shredded cabbage
¼ cup grated carrots
¼ cup grated cheese (optional)

For the *chapatis*
1 cup whole wheat flour (*gehun ka atta*)
1 tsp oil
½ tsp salt

Other ingredients

Whole wheat flour (*gehun ka atta*) for rolling

For the soya rolls

½ cup soaked, boiled and drained chickpeas (*kabulichana*)
½ cup soya granules
¼ cup finely chopped mint (*phudina)*
1 tsp finely chopped green chillies
1 tsp finely chopped ginger
2 tsp oil
Salt to taste

Other ingredients

2 tsp oil for cooking

For the *chapatis*

1. Mix the flour, oil and salt and make a dough by adding enough warm water.
2. Knead the dough well and keep for ½ an hour. Knead again.
3. Divide into 6 portions and roll out each portion into 6" (150 mm.) diameter thin rounds with the help of a little whole wheat flour.
4. Cook lightly on both sides on a *tava* (griddle) and keep aside.

For the soya rolls
1. Soak the soya granules in hot water for 10 to 15 minutes. Drain and squeeze out all the water.
2. In a blender, blend the *kabuli chana*, soya granules, green chillies and ginger into a thick, coarse paste.
3. Add the mint and salt and mix well.
4. Divide the mixture into 6 equal portions and shape each portion into cylindrical rolls.
5. Heat the oil in a non-stick pan and cook the rolls on both sides till they are golden brown. Keep aside.

How to proceed
1. Place a *chapati* on a flat surface. Put a soya roll on one end of the *chapati* and spread ½ tbsp of chilli sauce over it.
2. Sprinkle some cabbage, carrots and cheese on top and roll it up tightly.
3. Repeat with remaining ingredients to make 5 more rolls.
4. Place the *chapati* rolls on a hot *tava* (griddle) and cook using a little oil till they turn golden brown. Serve hot.

Nutritive values per roll

Energy	Protein	Carbohydrates	Fat	Calcium	Folic Acid
145 cal	5.6 gm	19.6 gm	4.9 gm	40.8 mg	27.1 mcg

Nutritious Idlis

Rich in
Folic Acid
& Fibre

A sneaky way to get your children to eat more greens and fibre is to give them nutritious idlis pepped up with vegetables.

Preparation time: 20 minutes.   Cooking time: 30 minutes.   Serves 6.

For the *idli* batter
1½ cups broken wheat (*daliya*)
1½ cups semolina (*rawa/ sooji*)
¼ cup *chana dal* (split Bengal gram)
¼ cup *urad dal* (split black lentils)
2 cups curds (*dahi*)
1 tsp baking powder
Salt to taste

For the vegetable mixture
1 cup grated carrots
¼ cup chopped French beans
¼ cup coarsely mashed green peas

24

½ tsp mustard seeds (*rai/sarson*)
A pinch asafoetida (*hing*)
1 tsp finely chopped green chillies
½ tsp ginger paste
¼ cup finely chopped onions
½ cup chopped coriander
Salt to taste

Other ingredient
½ tsp oil for greasing

For the *idli* batter
1. Dry roast the broken wheat and semolina on a *tava* (griddle) till they are golden brown in colour. Remove and keep aside in a bowl.
2. Dry roast the *chana dal* and *urad dal*. Add ½ cup of water and allow to cook on a slow flame till they are tender.
3. Mash the *dals* lightly and add to the broken wheat and semolina.
4. Add all the remaining ingredients and enough lukewarm water to make *idli* batter. Keep aside.

For the vegetable mixture
1. Heat the oil in a small pan and add the mustard seeds to it. When they crackle, add the asafoetida, green chillies and ginger paste.
2. Add the onions and sauté till they turn golden brown.
3. Add the carrots, French beans, green peas, salt and a little water and cook covered till the vegetables are tender and the mixture is dry.
4. Switch off the flame and add the coriander. Mix well and keep aside.

How to proceed
1. Grease an 200 mm. (8") *thali* with oil and spread half the *idli* batter in it.
2. Add a layer of the vegetable mixture.
3. Top with the remaining half of the *idli* batter.
4. Steam in a steamer for about 20 minutes. Cool and cut into pieces. Remove from the mould and serve hot.

Nutritive values per serving

Energy	Protein	Carbohydrates	Fat	Folic Acid	Fibre
397 cal	13.2 gm	69.3 gm	5.9 gm	**27.0 mcg**	**1.4 gm**

Nutritious Burger

Rich in
Iron &
Folic Acid

Shallow fried paneer tikkis make this a low-fat, healthy version of the fat-laden burger.

Preparation time: 15 minutes.   Cooking time: 10 minutes.   Makes 6 burgers.

6 brown bread buns
12 lettuce leaves
6 onion slices
12 cucumber slices
12 tomato slices
2 tsp tomato ketchup mixed with 1 tsp chilli sauce (optional)
Salt to taste

For the cheese sauce
2 cheese slices
¼ cup milk

For the *paneer phudina tikkis*
½ cup grated *paneer* (cottage cheese)
½ cup boiled, peeled and mashed potatoes
4 tbsp finely chopped mint (*phudina*)
2 green chillies, finely chopped
2 to 3 tsp cornflour
Salt to taste

For the cheese sauce
1. Heat the milk in a pan, add the cheese slices to it and cook on a slow flame till the cheese melts.
2. Remove from the fire and keep aside.

For the *paneer phudina tikkis*
1. Combine all the ingredients in a bowl and mix well. Divide mixture into 6 equal portions.
2. Shape each portion into a round and flatten slightly to make *tikkis*.
3. Cook them on a non-stick pan using a little oil till both sides are golden brown. Keep aside.

How to proceed

1. Horizontally slice each bun into two and toast lightly in a pre-heated oven or on a *tava* (griddle).
2. Apply a little cheese sauce and some tomato ketchup on both the halves of the bun.
3. On one half of the bun arrange 2 lettuce leaves, a *tikki*, an onion slice, 2 cucumber slices and 2 tomato slices.
4. Sprinkle a little salt and cover with the other half of the bun.
5. Repeat with the remaining ingredients to make 5 more burgers.
   Serve immediately.

Nutritive values per burger

Energy	Protein	Carbohydrates	Fat	Iron	Folic Acid
244 cal	9.8 gm	35.6 gm	6.8 gm	3.4 mg	26.7 mcg

Russian Salad Bread Cups

Rich in Calcium, Zinc & Fibre

These nutritious little cups of bread hold a medley of colourful vegetables and fruits.

Preparation time: 15 minutes.   Cooking time: 15 minutes.   Serves 4.
Baking temperature: 200°C (400°F).   Baking time: 15 minutes.

For the toast cases
8 slices whole wheat bread
2 tsp butter

For the Russian salad filling (makes approx. 1½ cups)
¼ cup chopped boiled, peeled and chopped potatoes
¼ cup boiled green peas
2 tbsp peeled, chopped and boiled carrots
2 tbsp chopped and boiled French beans
2 tbsp peeled and chopped pineapple
2 tbsp chopped apple
2 tbsp chopped lettuce
2 tbsp eggless mayonnaise
1 tbsp fresh cream

Salt and freshly ground pepper to taste

For the toast cases
1. Slice off the crust from the bread slices.
2. Wrap the bread slices in a muslin cloth and steam in a pressure cooker for 5 to 7 minutes.
3. Flatten the bread slices and press each bread slice into the cavities of a muffin tray greased with butter.
4. Brush some melted butter over them and bake in a pre-heated oven at 200°C (400°F) for 10 minutes or until crisp. Demould and keep aside.

For the Russian salad filling
1. Mix all the ingredients in a bowl.
2. Divide into 8 equal portions and keep aside.

How to proceed
Fill a portion of the mixture in each toast case. Serve immediately.

Handy tip: Muffin trays are used for making cup cakes, muffins etc. They are available at any shop which sells cake moulds.

Nutritive values per serving

Energy	Protein	Carbohydrates	Fat	Calcium	Zinc	Fibre
210 cal	5.6 gm	33.8 gm	6.2 gm	33.6 mg	0.9 mg	1.3 gm

Rosti Pizzas

Rich in
Calcium,
Folic Acid
& Fibre

Mozzarella cheese and colourful vegetables help make this low fat potato snack as appealing as a regular pizza.

Preparation time: 15 minutes.   Cooking time: 15 minutes.   Serves 8.
Baking temperature: 200°C (400°F).   Baking time: 20 minutes.

4 medium potatoes
½ cup chopped onions
1 tsp finely chopped green chillies
2 cups boiled mixed vegetables (broccoli, corn, baby corn, etc.), cut into cubes
½ tsp dried oregano
¼ cup fresh cream
¼ cup grated mozzarella cheese
2 tsp butter
Salt and freshly ground pepper to taste

For the tomato sauce
4 large tomatoes

1 bayleaf (*tejpatta*)
4 to 6 peppercorns
½ cup finely chopped onions
1 tsp chopped garlic
2 tsp sugar
½ tsp dried oregano
1 tbsp olive oil or oil
Salt to taste

Other ingredients
Oil for greasing

For the tomato sauce
1. Put the tomatoes in a vesselful of boiling water for 10 minutes.
2. Peel, cut into quarters and deseed the tomatoes.
3. Chop finely and keep the tomato pulp aside.
4. Heat the olive oil in a pan, add the bayleaf and peppercorns and sauté for a few seconds.
5. Add the onions and garlic and sauté for a few minutes.
6. Add the tomato pulp and allow it to simmer for 10 to 15 minutes until the sauce reduces a little.

7. Add the sugar and salt and simmer for some more time.
8. Finally, add the oregano and mix well. Remove the bayleaf and peppercorns and discard. Keep aside.

How to proceed
1. Parboil the potatoes peel and allow them to cool.
2. Heat a small non-stick pan, add the butter and sauté the onions and green chillies.
3. Grease a 250 mm. diameter baking dish and spread the sautéed onions and green chillies at the base.
4. Sprinkle a little salt and pepper and then grate the potatoes evenly over it.
5. Arrange a layer of vegetables over the potato layer and sprinkle salt, pepper and oregano over it.
6. Pour the tomato sauce over the vegetable layer and finally a layer of cream.
7. Top with cheese and bake in a pre-heated oven for about 15 minutes. Serve hot.

Nutritive values per serving

Energy	Protein	Carbohydrates	Fat	Calcium	Folic Acid	Fibre
141 cal	3.4 gm	18.5 gm	6.2 gm	73.9 mg	29.6 mcg	1.2 gm

Paushtic Parathas

Picture on page 37.

Get your kids to eat unpopular vegetables by disguising them in these nutritious parathas.

Preparation time: 10 minutes.   Cooking time: 20 minutes.   Makes 8 parathas.

1½ cups whole wheat flour (*gehun ka atta*)
¼ cup *besan* (Bengal gram flour)
¾ cup peeled, boiled and grated potatoes
1 cup chopped spinach (*palak*)
¼ cup grated carrots
2 tsp finely chopped green chillies
4 tbsp fresh curds (*dahi*)
2 tsp oil
Salt of taste

Other ingredients
Whole wheat flour (*gehun ka atta*) for rolling
1 tsp oil for cooking

1. Mix all the ingredients and make a soft and smooth dough.
2. Divide the dough into 8 equal portions and roll out each portion into triangles with the help of a little whole wheat flour.
3. Cook on a non-stick *tava* (griddle) using a little oil on both sides till they turn golden brown.
   Serve hot.

Nutritive values per paratha

Energy	Protein	Carbohydrates	Fat	Iron	Folic Acid
111 cal	3.6 gm	18.6 gm	2.3 gm	**1.3 mg**	**23.8 mcg**

PAUSHTIC PARATHAS : Recipe on the page 35. →